Essential Guide to Writing

Writing Avenue

Michael A. Putlack

Essay Writing

5

DARAKWON

About the Author

Michael A. Putlack

MA in History, Tufts University, Medford, MA, USA

More than two decades of experience as a writer, editor, and proofreader

Expert test developer of TOEFL, TOEIC, and TEPS

The author of the *Fundamental Reading Plus* series and *Reading Voyage Starter* 2, 3

Essential Guide to Writing

Writing Avenue 5

Essay Writing

Publisher Chung Kyudo
Author Michael A. Putlack
Editors Seo Jeong-ah, Jeong Yeonsoon, Kim Mina, Kim Mikyeong
Designers Park Narae, Forest

First published in March 2021
By Darakwon, Inc.
Darakwon Bldg., 211, Munbal-ro, Paju-si, Gyeonggi-do 10881
Republic of Korea
Tel: 82-2-736-2031 (Ext. 250)
Fax: 82-2-732-2037

ISBN 978-89-277-0451-5 54740
978-89-277-0446-1 54740 (set)

www.darakwon.co.kr

Photo Credits
Ferenc Szelepcsenyi (p.14, w_p.6), mama_mia (p.21), Julie Clopper (p.21), Koshiro K (p.24, w_p.6), Sky Motion (p.26), Il.studio (p.26), Alexey Boldin (p.27), SIAATH (p.31), Nicole Kwiatkowski (p.34), Takashi Images (p.36), s_bukley (p.44), Featureflash Photo Agency (p.44), landmarkmedia (p.44, w_p.14), Gabriela Bertolini (p.46), Anton_Ivanov (p.46), Life In Pixels (p.47), Fotos593 (p.72) / www.shutterstock.com

Components Main Book / Workbook
10 9 8 7 6 5 4   24 25 26 27 28

Essential Guide to Writing

Writing Avenue

Essay Writing

5

Table of Contents

Unit	Topic	Writing Goal	Type of Writing
Unit 1	My Future	To write about my bucket list	Narrative Essay
Unit 2	My Favorite Website	To write about my favorite website	Descriptive Essay
Unit 3	My Most Memorable Trip	To write about my most memorable trip	Narrative Essay
Unit 4	Famous People	To write about a famous person and what makes that person famous	Expository Essay
Unit 5	If I Were...	To write about an imaginary situation	Narrative Essay
Unit 6	Taking Online Classes	To write about my preference between two choices	Persuasive Essay
Unit 7	The Environment	To write about human activities and how they affect the environment	Expository Essay
Unit 8	Mobile Phones at Schools	To write about whether I agree or disagree with a statement	Persuasive Essay

How to Use This Book

• *Student Book*

1. Before You Write

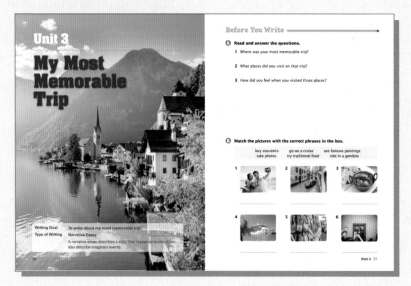

Thinking about the Topic
Three warm-up questions help readers think about the writing topic.

Previewing the Key Expressions
Readers can learn the key expressions by matching the phrases with the pictures or by filling in the table.

2. Analyzing the Model Essay

QR code for listening to the model essay

Reading the Model Essay
Readers can read an example of the essay topic and use it as a template when they write their essay.

Answering Questions
Several questions about the model essay are provided. By answering them, readers can learn the topic of the essay and what important details are included.

Completing the Brainstorming and Outlining
By completing the brainstorming and outlining, readers can review the model essay and learn how the essay is structured.

3. Collecting Ideas

Getting Ideas from Collecting Ideas

Ideas related to the writing topic are provided. Readers can brainstorm and learn new ideas before writing their drafts.

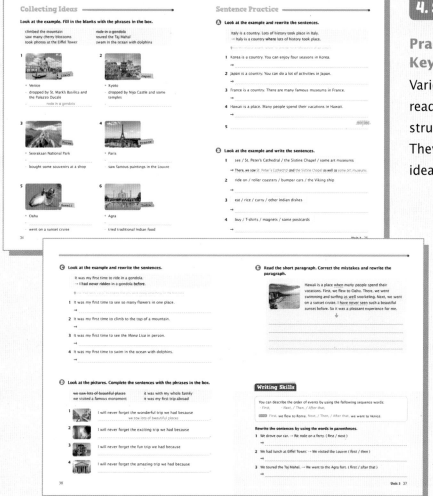

4. Sentence Practice

Practicing Sentences with Key Structures

Various types of questions allow readers to practice the key structures of the model essay. They also help readers gather ideas before writing.

Correcting a Short Paragraph

Readers can check if they understand the key structures they learned by correcting the mistakes in the short paragraph.

5. Writing Skills

Readers learn various phrases and expressions that can help them improve their writing skills.

6. Brainstorming & Outlining

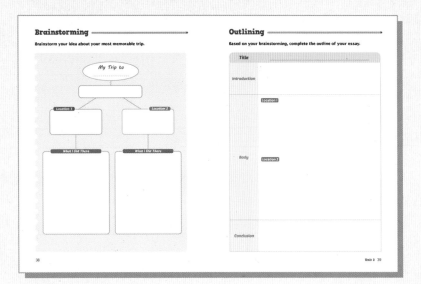

Brainstorming
Readers can come up with ideas about the essay topic.

Outlining
By making an outline, readers can organize their ideas and structure their essays to have an introduction, a body, and a conclusion. Then, they can write, revise, edit the first draft, and write the final draft in the workbook.

Vocabulary and Structure Review
Readers can review the key vocabulary they learned in each unit by writing the meaning of each word and phrase. They can also review the key structures in the unit.

• Workbook

7. More Questions
Readers can practice and review the key structures. They can also write sentences from the model essay by matching the phrases.

8. First Draft ➔ Final Draft
By using the outline, readers can write their first drafts. After revising and editing their drafts, readers can write their final drafts.

About Essay Writing

1. What Is an Essay?

An essay is a short work of writing that is often personal and nonfiction in nature. An essay often describes, argues, explains, or analyzes a particular subject. In an essay, the writer may use facts or personal arguments to make a point.

2. What Does an Essay Consist Of?

An essay consists of three main parts: an introduction, a body, and a conclusion.

- The introduction is the first paragraph of the essay. It introduces the topic of the essay. It also has a thesis statement, which is the main idea of the essay.
- The body is the main part of the essay. It is made up of one or more paragraphs. Each body paragraph has a topic sentence and supporting details.
- The conclusion is the final paragraph of the essay. It summarizes the main points of the essay and restates the thesis.

Introduction   **Ducksters: My Favorite Website**   **Thesis Statement**

I use the Internet all the time, so I visit many websites. The website that I like more than any others is called Ducksters.

Ducksters is a website focusing on education. So it has articles on various topics. Some of them are history, science, and geography. I have been visiting Duksters for many years. I love to read the articles and to learn new things there.

Another reason that I like Duksters is that it has lots of games. Many of them are learning games. So I can improve my math and verbal skills while I also have fun.

In my opinion, Duksters is one of the best websites on the Internet. If you want to learn and have fun, you should check out the website.

Body   **Conclusion**

3. What Are the Types of Essays?

1) Expository Essay

It gives information about a topic or explains how to do something.

2) Narrative Essay

It describes a story that happened to you. It can also describe imaginary events.

3) Persuasive Essay

It encourages readers to make a choice by providing evidence and examples.

4) Descriptive Essay

It describes a person, place, or thing. It shows what the person, location, or object is like.

Unit 1

My Future

Writing Goal	To write about my bucket list
Type of Writing	Narrative Essay
	A narrative essay describes a story that happened to you. It can also describe imaginary events.

Before You Write

A **Read and answer the questions.**

1 Do you have a bucket list?

2 What are some activities you would like to do in the future?

3 Where do you need to go to do those activities?

B **Match the pictures with the correct phrases in the box.**

| go scuba diving | see the Northern Lights | play the clarinet |
| star in a movie | go on a safari | climb a mountain |

1
_____

2
_____

3
_____

4
_____

5
_____

6
_____

Analyzing the Model Essay

 Read the model essay and answer the questions.

My Bucket List

A bucket list is a list of things a person wants to do before dying. Today at school, my teacher told my class about her bucket list. There were ten items on her list. I thought that was interesting. As a result, I decided to make my own bucket list.

First, what I am interested in is scuba diving. I would love to go scuba diving in the Caribbean Sea. It has many beautiful coral reefs, so I could see all kinds of tropical fish. I might even see a shark.

Another one of my dreams is to see the Northern Lights in Norway. I became fascinated by them when I saw them on a TV program last year. I think seeing them from the Arctic Circle would be amazing.

So far, those are the only two items on my bucket list. I will keep thinking of others though.

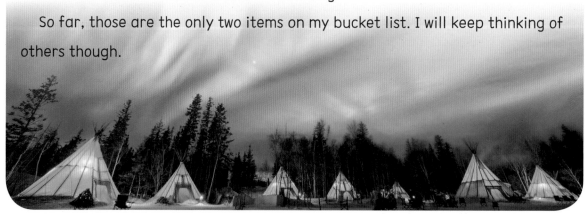

1 What is the essay about?

_____

2 Where are two places the writer would like to visit?

_____

3 What does the writer want to do in each place?

1) _____

2) _____

B **Read the model essay again and complete the brainstorming and outlining.**

My Bucket List

Activity 1

_____ in the Caribbean Sea

- has many _____
- see all kinds of _____
- even see _____

Activity 2

_____ in Norway

- saw them on a TV program
  → became _____
- seeing them from _____
  → amazing

	Title _____
Introduction	• a bucket list: a list of things a person _____ • decided to _____
Body	**Activity 1** would love to _____ • it has many beautiful coral reefs • could _____ • might even _____ **Activity 2** want to _____ • became fascinated when I _____ last year • seeing them from the Arctic Circle _____
Conclusion	• the _____ on my bucket list • will keep thinking of others

Collecting Ideas

Look at the example. Fill in the blanks with the phrases in the box.

play in an orchestra	~~see tropical fish~~
has lots of national parks	meet the president
visit a snow-covered mountain	perform for millions of people

Activity 1

1

- go scuba diving in the Caribbean Sea
- has many coral reefs
- _____ see tropical fish

2

- go on a safari in Kenya
- _____
- see lions, zebras, and other large animals

3

• _____
- has lots of power
- meet many leaders of other countries

Activity 2

4

- star in a movie
- watched some documentaries on movies
- _____

5

- play the clarinet
- went to a music concert
- _____

6

- climb the world's highest mountain
- read a book about a mountain climber
- _____

Sentence Practice

A **Look at the pictures. Write the sentences with the words and phrases in the box.**

Africa	mountain climbing	~~scuba diving~~	leaders

💡 The relative pronoun "what" means "the thing which."

1 **What I am interested in is** scuba diving. _____

2 _____

3 _____

4 _____

5 Your Idea _____

B **Look at the example and complete the sentences.**

~~see all kinds of tropical fish~~	play the clarinet in it
see lions, zebras, and other large animals	visit a snow-covered mountain

1 It has many beautiful coral reefs, _____**so I could** see all kinds of tropical fish_____ .

2 It has lots of national parks, _____ .

3 The area has beautiful scenery, _____ .

4 The orchestra has many musicians, _____ .

C Look at the pictures. Complete the sentences with the words and phrases in the boxes.

~~see~~	meet	~~the Northern Lights~~	a movie
play	star in	the president	the clarinet

💡 A "to-infinitive" phrase can be a subject complement after "be."

1 Another one of my dreams is ___**to see** the Northern Lights___ .

2 Another one of my dreams is _____ .

3 Another one of my dreams is _____ .

4 Another one of my dreams is _____ .

5 Your Idea _____

D Look at the example and write the sentences.

1 (see them from the Arctic Circle / amazing)

→ **I think seeing** them from the Arctic Circle **would be** amazing.

2 (play in an orchestra / wonderful)

→ _____

3 (visit a snow-covered mountain / exciting)

→ _____

4 (perform for millions of people / a dream come true)

→ _____

E **Read the short paragraph. Correct the mistakes and rewrite the paragraph.**

 I decided to make my own bucket list. First, <u>where</u> I am interested in is mountain climbing. Another one of my dreams is <u>play</u> the clarinet. I think playing in an orchestra would <u>being</u> exciting.

_____

_____

_____

_____

Writing Skills

After you make a statement, you can give a result of that statement by writing:

· *As a result,*   · *Therefore,*

Example I thought that was interesting. As a result, / Therefore, I decided to make my own bucket list.

Rewrite the sentences by using the words in parentheses.

1 I thought that was thrilling. I went on the roller coaster again. (as a result)

→ _____

2 I thought that was fun. I tried to learn how to water-ski. (therefore)

→ _____

Brainstorming

Brainstorm your idea about your bucket list.

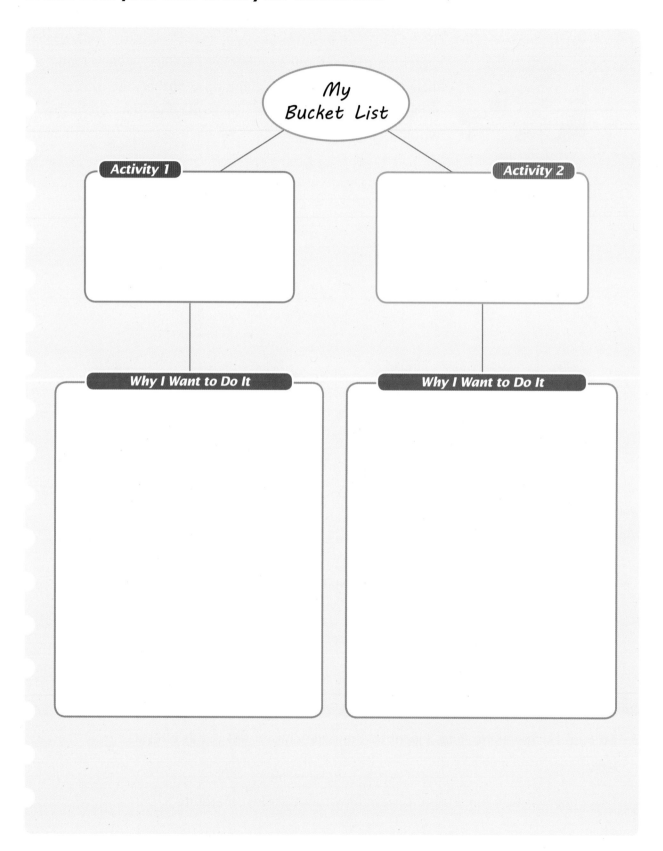

My
Bucket List

Activity 1

Activity 2

Why I Want to Do It

Why I Want to Do It

Outlining

Based on your brainstorming, complete the outline of your essay.

Title	
Introduction	
Body	**Activity 1**
	Activity 2
Conclusion	

Unit 2

My Favorite Website

Writing Goal	To write about my favorite website
Type of Writing	Descriptive Essay

A descriptive essay describes a person, place, or thing. It shows the reader what the person, location, or object is like.

Before You Write

A **Read and answer the questions.**

1 Do you have a favorite website?

2 What kind of website is it?

3 What do you do when you visit that website?

B **Match the pictures with the correct phrases in the box.**

> read articles   read book reviews   watch and share videos
> shop online   post photos   search for information

1

_____

2

_____

3

_____

4

_____

5

_____

6

_____

Analyzing the Model Essay

 Read the model essay and answer the questions.

Ducksters: My Favorite Website

I use the Internet all the time, so I visit many websites. The website that I like more than any others is called Ducksters.

Ducksters is a website focusing on education. So it has articles on various topics. Some of them are history, science, and geography. I have been visiting Ducksters for many years. I love to read the articles and to learn new things there.

Another reason that I like Ducksters is that it has lots of games. Many of them are learning games. So I can improve my math and verbal skills while I also have fun.

In my opinion, Ducksters is one of the best websites on the Internet. If you want to learn and have fun, you should check out the website.

1 What is the writer's favorite website? What kind of website it is?

_____

2 What does the writer love to do on the website?

_____

3 How can the website help the writer?

_____

B **Read the model essay again and complete the brainstorming and outlining.**

Ducksters:
My Favorite Website

Reason 1

a website focusing on
_____

- has _____ on various topics
- _____ and learn new things

Reason 2

has lot of _____

- are learning games
- improve _____ while having fun

	Title _____
Introduction	• visit many websites • like _____ more than any others
Body	**Reason 1** is a website _____ • has _____ → some of them are history, science, and geography • love to read the articles and to _____ there **Reason 2** has _____ • many of them are _____ • can _____ while I also have fun
Conclusion	• Ducksters: one of the _____ on the Internet • if you want to _____ → check out the website

Collecting Ideas

Look at the example. Fill in the blanks with the phrases in the box.

~~has lots of games~~	search for information
post and share photos	ships to over 100 countries
stay updated on the latest books	watch, upload, and share videos

1

Ducksters

- focuses on education
- has articles on various topics
- <u>has lots of games</u>

2

Google

- focuses on online searches
- _____
- has an email service

3

YouTube

- focuses on sharing videos
- _____
- can learn anything by watching videos

4

Instagram

- focuses on sharing photos
- _____
- has filters to make photos more beautiful

5

Amazon.com

- focuses on online shopping
- shop online
- _____

6

Goodreads

- focuses on books
- _____
- can read book reviews

Sentence Practice

A **Look at the example and write the sentences.**

(Ducksters / education)
→ Ducksters **is a website focusing on** education.

💡 A present participle (verb-ing) phrase comes after a noun and modifies the noun like an adjective.

1 (Google / online searches)

→ _____

2 (Goodreads / books)

→ _____

3 (Instagram / sharing photos)

→ _____

4 (Amazon.com / online shopping)

→ _____

B **Look at the example and write the sentences.**

💡 Use "have/has been + verb-ing" to make the present perfect continuous.

1 | visit / Ducksters / for many years |

→ **I have been visiting** Ducksters for many years.

2 | use / Google / for a long time |

→ _____

3 | post / on Instagram / for three years |

→ _____

4 | make / videos for YouTube / since 2019 |

→ _____

C **Look at the example and write the sentences.**

> it has lots of games
> it ships to over 100 countries
>
> I can read book reviews
> I can learn anything by watching videos

1 (Ducksters)

→ **Another reason that I like** Ducksters **is that** it has lots of games.

2 (YouTube)

→ _____

3 (Amazon.com)

→ _____

4 (Goodreads)

→ _____

Your Idea

5 _____

D **Look at the pictures. Complete the sentences with the phrases in the box.**

> learn and have fun
> share your life with other people
>
> get the latest news on books
> do online searches and use email

1   **If you want to** learn and have fun _____,
you should check out the website.

2    _____,
you should check out the website.

3    _____,
you should check out the website.

4   _____,
you should check out the website.

E **Read the short paragraph. Correct the mistakes and rewrite the paragraph.**

YouTube is a website focus on sharing videos. So it has all kinds of videos to watch. I have been posted videos on YouTube since 2019. In my opinion, YouTube is one of the best website on the Internet.

↓

_____

_____

_____

_____

Writing Skills

You can express your opinions by using the following words:

· *In my opinion,*　　· *I believe (that)*

Example In my opinion, / I believe (that) Ducksters is one of the best websites on the Internet.

Write the sentences by using the words in parentheses.

1 (Google / one of the most useful websites on the Internet / in my opinion)

　→ _____

2 (Instagram / one of the greatest websites on the Internet / I believe)

　→ _____

Brainstorming

Brainstorm your ideas about your favorite website.

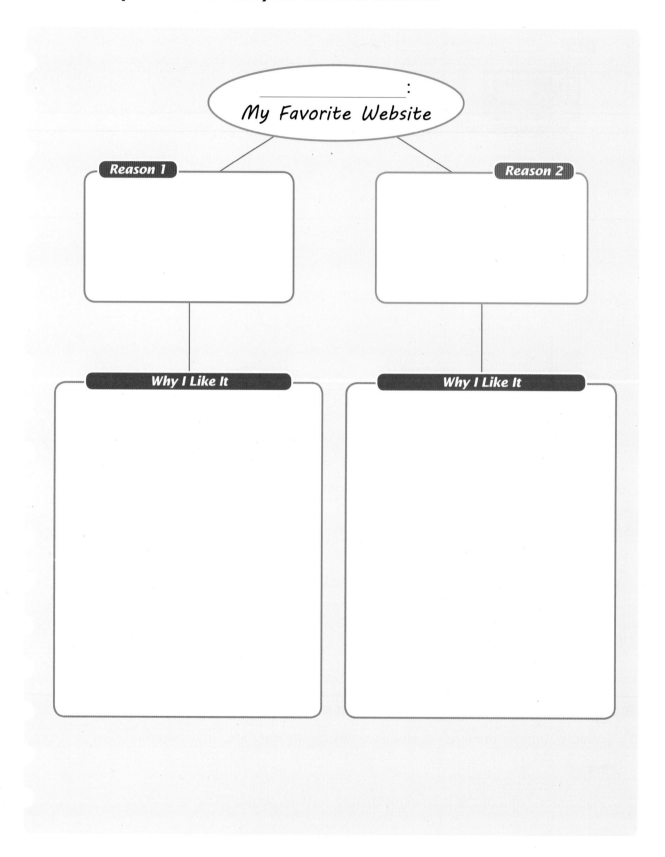

My Favorite Website

Reason 1

Reason 2

Why I Like It

Why I Like It

Outlining

Based on your brainstorming, complete the outline of your essay.

Title	
Introduction	
Body	**Reason 1**
	Reason 2
Conclusion	

Unit 3

My Most Memorable Trip

Writing Goal	To write about my most memorable trip
Type of Writing	Narrative Essay
	A narrative essay describes a story that happened to you. It can also describe imaginary events.

Before You Write

A **Read and answer the questions.**

1 Where was your most memorable trip?

2 What places did you visit on that trip?

3 How did you feel when you visited those places?

B **Match the pictures with the correct phrases in the box.**

buy souvenirs   go on a cruise   see famous paintings
take photos   try traditional food   ride in a gondola

1

2

3

4

5

6

Analyzing the Model Essay

A **Read the model essay and answer the questions.**

My Trip to Italy

Last summer, I traveled to Italy with my family. It was my first trip to Italy, so I was very excited.

Italy is a country where lots of history took place. First, we flew to Rome. It was the capital of the ancient Roman Empire. In Rome, we visited the Pantheon and the Catacombs. We also went to the Vatican. There, we saw St. Peter's Cathedral and the Sistine Chapel as well as some art museums.

Next, we went to Venice, one of my favorite cities. We dropped by St. Mark's Basilica and the Palazzo Ducale. We also rode in a gondola. I had never ridden in a gondola before. So it was a new experience for me.

I will never forget the wonderful trip we had because we saw lots of beautiful places. I would also love to return one day since the cities were so wonderful.

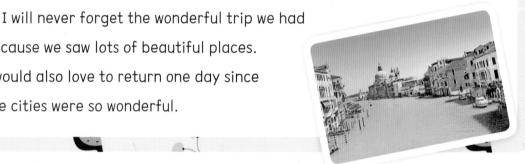

1 What is the essay about?

_____

2 What cities did the writer visit?

_____

3 Why does the writer want to return one day?

_____

B **Read the model essay again and complete the brainstorming and outlining.**

My Trip to Italy

last summer, with _____

Location 1
Rome

Location 2
_____

- the Pantheon and _____
- _____ → saw St. Peter's Cathedral, the Sistine Chapel, and some art museums

- St. Mark's Basilica and the Palazzo Ducale
- _____

	Title _____
Introduction	• last summer, with my family • was _____ → was very excited
Body	**Location 1** flew to Rome, _____ • visited _____ • also went to _____ → saw _____ **Location 2** went to Venice, _____ • dropped by _____ • also _____ → was a new experience
Conclusion	• will never forget because we _____ • would love to return since the cities _____

Collecting Ideas

Look at the example. Fill in the blanks with the phrases in the box.

climbed the mountain	~~rode in a gondola~~
saw many cherry blossoms	toured the Taj Mahal
took photos at the Eiffel Tower	swam in the ocean with dolphins

1

- Venice
  - dropped by St. Mark's Basilica and the Palazzo Ducale
  - ___rode in a gondola___

2

- Kyoto
  - dropped by Nijo Castle and some temples
  - _____

3

- Seoraksan National Park
  - _____
  - bought some souvenirs at a shop

4

- Paris
  - _____
  - saw famous paintings in the Louvre

5

- Oahu
  - _____
  - went on a sunset cruise

6

- Agra
  - _____
  - tried traditional Indian food

Sentence Practice

A **Look at the example and rewrite the sentences.**

Italy is a country. Lots of history took place in Italy.
→ Italy is a country **where** lots of history took place.

Use the relative adverb "where" to provide more information about a place.

1 Korea is a country. You can enjoy four seasons in Korea.

→ _____

2 Japan is a country. You can do a lot of activities in Japan.

→ _____

3 France is a country. There are many famous museums in France.

→ _____

4 Hawaii is a place. Many people spend their vacations in Hawaii.

→ _____

Your Idea

5 _____

B **Look at the example and write the sentences.**

1 see / St. Peter's Cathedral / the Sistine Chapel / some art museums

→ **There, we saw** St. Peter's Cathedral **and** the Sistine Chapel **as well as** some art museums.

2 ride on / roller coasters / bumper cars / the Viking ship

→ _____

3 eat / rice / curry / other Indian dishes

→ _____

4 buy / T-shirts / magnets / some postcards

→ _____

C Look at the example and rewrite the sentences.

It was my first time to ride in a gondola.
→ **I had never ridden** in a gondola **before.**

💡 Use "had never + p.p." to explain that you were doing something for the first time.

1 It was my first time to see so many flowers in one place.

→ _____

2 It was my first time to climb to the top of a mountain.

→ _____

3 It was my first time to see the *Mona Lisa* in person.

→ _____

4 It was my first time to swim in the ocean with dolphins.

→ _____

D Look at the pictures. Complete the sentences with the phrases in the box.

~~we saw lots of beautiful places~~   it was with my whole family
we visited a famous monument   it was my first trip abroad

1  I will never forget the wonderful trip we had because
_____ we saw lots of beautiful places _____ .

2  I will never forget the exciting trip we had because

_____ .

3  I will never forget the fun trip we had because

_____ .

4  I will never forget the amazing trip we had because

_____ .

E **Read the short paragraph. Correct the mistakes and rewrite the paragraph.**

Hawaii is a place <u>when</u> many people spend their vacations. First, we flew to Oahu. There, we went swimming and surfing <u>as well</u> snorkeling. Next, we went on a sunset cruise. <u>I have never seen</u> such a beautiful sunset before. So it was a pleasant experience for me.

↓

_____

_____

_____

_____

Writing Skills

You can describe the order of events by using the following sequence words:

· *First,*   · *Next, / Then, / After that,*

Example First, we flew to Rome. Next, / Then, / After that, we went to Venice.

Rewrite the sentences by using the information and words in parentheses.

1 (We drove our car. → We rode on a ferry.) (first / next)

→ _____

2 (We had lunch at the Eiffel Tower. → We visited the Louvre.) (first / then)

→ _____

3 (We toured the Taj Mahal. → We went to the Agra fort.) (first / after that)

→ _____

Brainstorming

Brainstorm your idea about your most memorable trip.

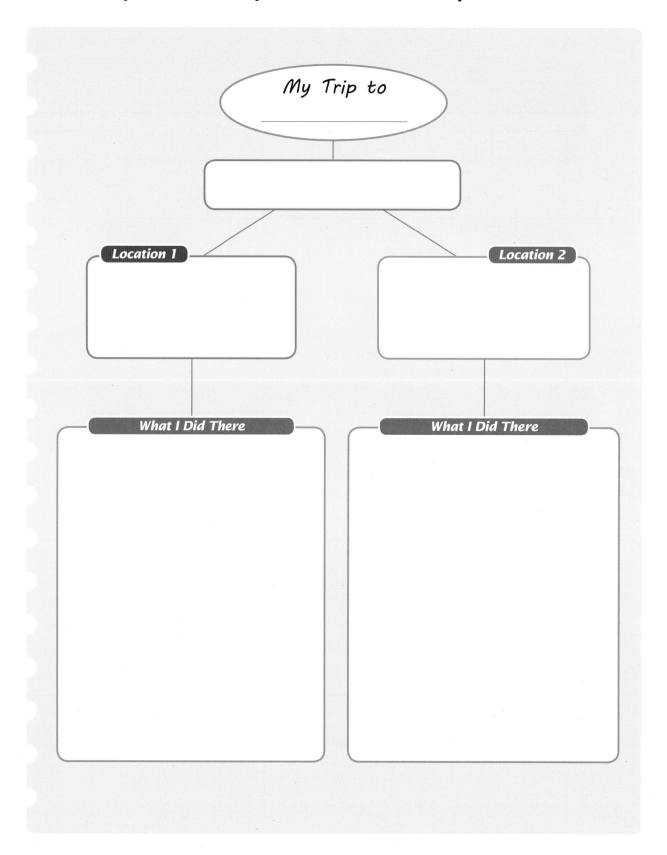

My Trip to

Location 1

Location 2

What I Did There

What I Did There

Outlining

Based on your brainstorming, complete the outline of your essay.

Title	
Introduction	
Body	**Location 1**
	Location 2
Conclusion	

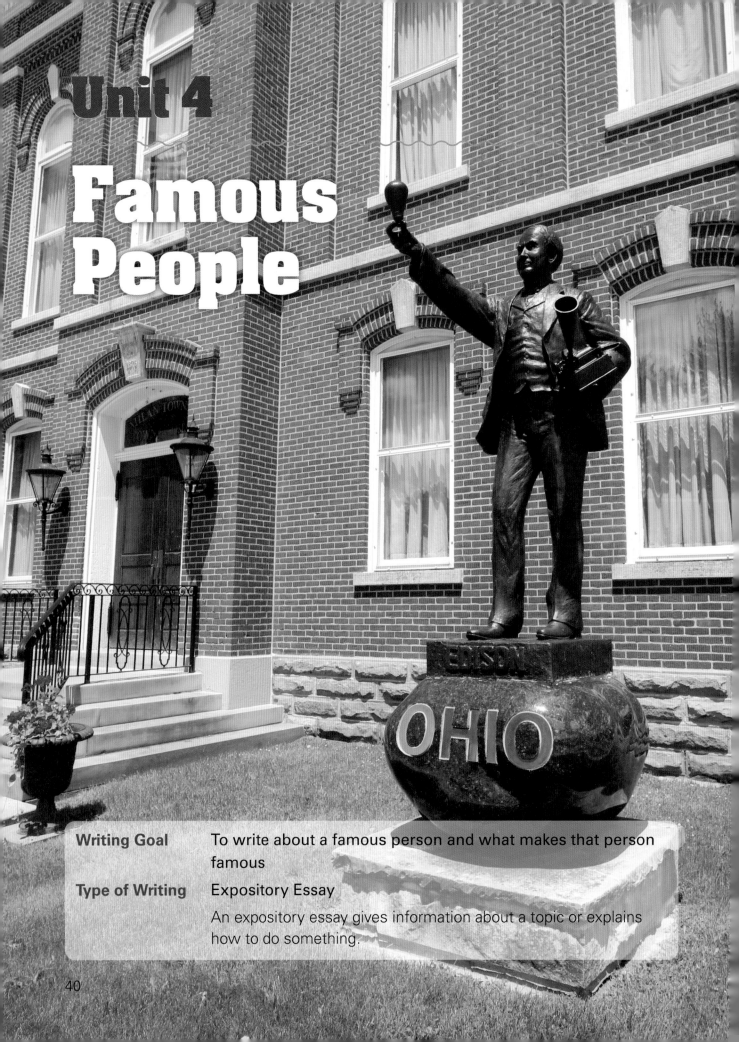

Unit 4

Famous People

Writing Goal	To write about a famous person and what makes that person famous
Type of Writing	Expository Essay
	An expository essay gives information about a topic or explains how to do something.

Before You Write

A **Read and answer the questions.**

1 Who is a famous person you admire?

2 What did that person do?

3 What characteristics helped make that person famous?

B **Fill in the chart with the words and phrases in the box.**

> Thomas Edison   Michelangelo   a great inventor   a successful author
> J.K. Rowling   a talented artist   Jim Carrey   a famous comedian and actor

Famous Person	Who He/She Is
• _____	• _____
• _____	• _____
• _____	• _____
• _____	• _____

Analyzing the Model Essay

A **Read the model essay and answer the questions.**

Thomas Edison

Thomas Edison was one of the world's greatest inventors. For a couple of reasons, he became a big success and got famous.

Edison did poorly at school, but he was always positive and never gave up. For instance, when he was trying to invent the light bulb, he failed 10,000 times. But he did not quit, so he finally succeeded. Because Edison never stopped trying, people around the world can enjoy indoor lighting.

He was also a very hardworking man. Edison enjoyed working all the time. During Edison's lifetime, he invented more than 1,000 items. One was the phonograph, which let people record sounds. Another was the motion picture camera, which people used to make movies.

Thomas Edison never quit and worked hard, too. Without a doubt, those two characteristics made him a great inventor and famous man. Whenever you think of inventors, you should think of Thomas Edison.

1 What is the essay about?

_____

2 What are two characteristics that helped Thomas Edison succeed?

1) _____

2) _____

3 What are two of the items that Thomas Edison invented?

_____

B **Read the model essay again and complete the brainstorming and outlining.**

Thomas Edison

Characteristic 1

positive, _____

- tried to invent the light bulb, but
_____
- never stopped trying
→ people can enjoy _____

Characteristic 2

very _____

- enjoyed _____
- invented more than 1,000 items
e.g. phonograph,
_____

	Title _____
Introduction	• Thomas Edison: one of the _____ • became _____ and got famous for a couple of reasons
Body	**Characteristic 1** was _____ and never gave up • tried to _____ but failed 10,000 times • never _____ → people can enjoy indoor lighting **Characteristic 2** was also _____ • _____ all the time • invented more than _____ e.g. _____ , _____
Conclusion	• _____ and _____ → made him _____ and famous man • whenever you think of _____ , think of Thomas Edison

Collecting Ideas

Look at the example. Fill in the blanks with the phrases in the box.

~~invented more than 1,000 items~~	won a large number of awards
worked hard to become a comedian	wrote the most popular children's books
learned a lot despite being deaf and blind	made many works of art

1

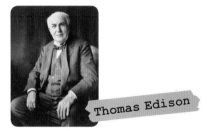

Thomas Edison

- an inventor
- was always positive and never gave up
- invented more than 1,000 items

2

Michelangelo

- an artist
- never stopped asking to study art
- _____

3

Helen Keller

- an author and educator
- _____
- inspired people and gave them hope

4

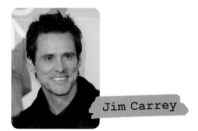

Jim Carrey

- a comedian and actor
- _____
- starred in many popular movies

5

J.K. Rowling

- an author
- did not quit writing despite having no job
- _____

6

Michael Jordan

- a basketball player
- practiced constantly to improve his skills
- _____

Sentence Practice

A **Look at the example and rewrite the sentences.**

> Thomas Edison was a great inventor.
> → Thomas Edison was **one of the world's greatest inventors.**

1 Michelangelo was a talented artist.

→ _____

2 J.K. Rowling is a successful author.

→ _____

3 Michael Jordan was a good basketball player.

→ _____

4 Jim Carrey is a famous comedian and actor.

→ _____

Your Idea

5 _____

B **Look at the example and complete the sentences.**

> ~~can enjoy indoor lighting~~   was able to improve his skills
> learned how to read and write   got the chance to be an artist

1 Because Edison never stopped trying, people ___can enjoy indoor lighting___ .

2 Because Michelangelo never stopped asking, he _____ .

3 Because Keller studied a lot with her teacher, she _____ .

4 Because Jordan practiced constantly, he _____ .

Your Idea

5 _____

C Look at the pictures. Complete the sentences with the phrases in the box.

is a sculpture	~~let people record sounds~~
was made into movies	showed he was the best player

💡 Use a comma if a relative clause gives extra information about the noun it modifies.

1 One was the phonograph, __which let people record sounds__ .

2 One was *David*, _____ .

3 One was the MVP award, _____ .

4 One was the *Harry Potter* series, _____ .

D Look at the example and write the sentences.

💡 "Whenever" means "every time that" or "any time that."

1 | inventors / Thomas Edison |

→ **Whenever you think of** inventors, **you should think of** Thomas Edison.

2 | artists / Michelangelo |

→ _____

3 | authors / J.K. Rowling |

→ _____

4 | comedians and actors / Jim Carrey |

→ _____

E **Read the short paragraph. Correct the mistakes and rewrite the paragraph.**

J.K Rowling is one of the most successful author. She did not have a job when she wrote *Harry Potter*. Because of she kept writing, she was able to publish her book. During her lifetime, she has written many books. One was the *Harry Potter and the Deathly Hallows*, that was the last book in the *Harry Potter* series.

↓

_____

_____

_____

_____

Writing Skills

When you want to emphasize a fact or opinion, you can write:
- *Without a doubt,*   - *Without question,*

Example Without a doubt, / Without question, those two characteristics made him a great inventor and famous man.

Rewrite the sentences by using the words in parentheses.

1 Michael Jordan was one of the greatest players in NBA history. (without a doubt)

→ _____

2 Helen Keller showed that disabled people could accomplish great things. (without question)

→ _____

Brainstorming

Brainstorm your idea about a famous person.

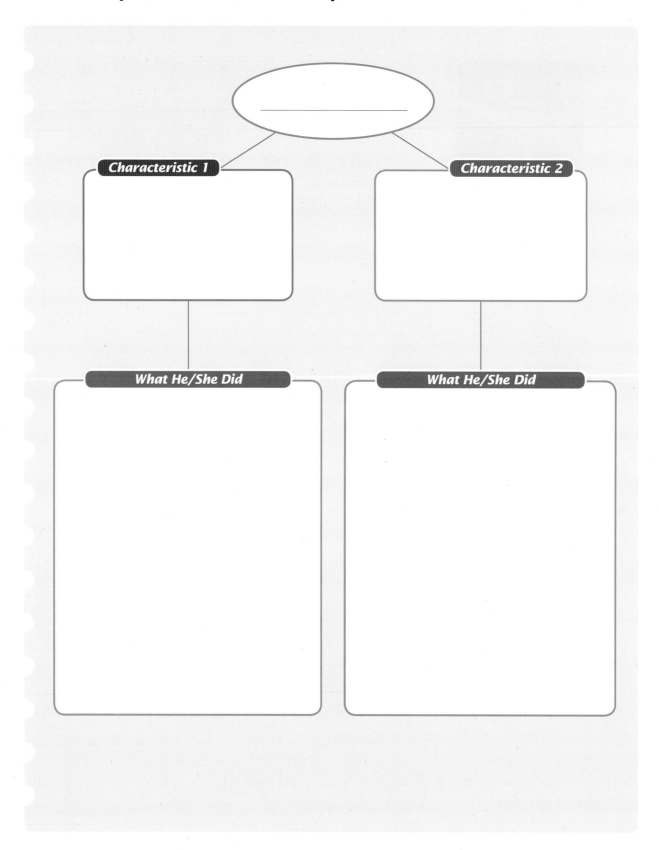

Outlining

Based on your brainstorming, complete the outline of your essay.

Title	
Introduction	
Body	**Characteristic 1** **Characteristic 2**
Conclusion	

Unit 5

If I Were...

Writing Goal	To write about an imaginary situation
Type of Writing	Narrative Essay
	A narrative essay describes a story that happened to you. It can also describe imaginary events.

Before You Write

A **Read and answer the questions.**

1 What would you like to be in the future?

2 What would you like to do if you were that person?

3 Why would you do those things?

B **Fill in the chart with the phrases in the box.**

treat the poor   a principal   a popular children's series   a doctor   my own private airplane   a writer   a rich person   get rid of

If I were...	I would...
• _____	• _____ school uniforms
• _____	• _____ for free
• _____	• write _____
• _____	• buy _____

Analyzing the Model Essay

 Read the model essay and answer the questions.

If I Were a Principal

I want to be a principal of a school. If I were a principal, I would make two big changes to help the students.

First, I would get rid of school uniforms. Many students complain about their uniforms and dislike wearing them. They would rather wear other clothes. If I got rid of school uniforms, the students would be happier.

Second, I would change the times school starts and ends. Most students have trouble waking up, so they often fall asleep during class. Others have a hard time paying attention. I would start school at 9:00 and finish at 4:00. Then, the students would be wide awake all day long.

Getting rid of school uniforms and changing the school times would improve the school a lot. As a principal, I would make those changes at once.

1 What is the essay about?

_____

2 What are the two changes the writer would make?

1) _____

2) _____

3 How would those changes help the students?

_____

B **Read the model essay again and complete the brainstorming and outlining.**

If I Were
a Principal

Plan 1
_____

- students _____ wearing them
- get rid of school uniforms
  → students would be _____

Plan 2

change the school times

- students have trouble _____
- start school _____ and finish _____
  → students would be _____ all day long

Title	_____	
Introduction	• want to be _____ • would _____ to help the students	
Body	**Plan 1** would _____ • students _____ and dislike wearing them • get rid of school uniforms → students would _____ **Plan 2** would change the times _____ • students have trouble waking up → _____ during class and have a hard time _____ • _____ at 9:00 and _____ at 4:00 → students would be _____	
Conclusion	_____ and _____ would improve the school a lot	

Collecting Ideas

Look at the example. Fill in the blanks with the phrases in the box.

travel in space	be a bestselling writer
~~change the school times~~	buy my own private airplane
try to find a cure for cancer	sell products around the world

1

Principal

- get rid of school uniforms
- change the school times

2

Astronaut

- _____
- talk to people about space

3

Writer

- write a popular children's series
- _____

4

Doctor

- treat the poor for free
- _____

5

CEO

- improve the quality of my company's products
- _____

6

A rich person

- build a nice house by the sea
- _____

Sentence Practice

A **Look at the example and write the sentences.**

💡 When you talk about untrue ideas in the present, use the past simple or "were" in the *if*-clause.

1 (a principal / make two big changes / help the students)

→ **If I were** a principal, **I would** make two big changes **to** help the students.

2 (a doctor / come up with two ways / treat my patients better)

→ _____

3 (a CEO / take two actions / improve my company)

→ _____

4 (an astronaut / do two things / improve our knowledge of science)

→ _____

Your Idea

5 _____

B **Look at the pictures. Write the sentences with the phrases in the box.**

treat the poor for free	travel in space
~~get rid of school uniforms~~	build a nice house by the sea

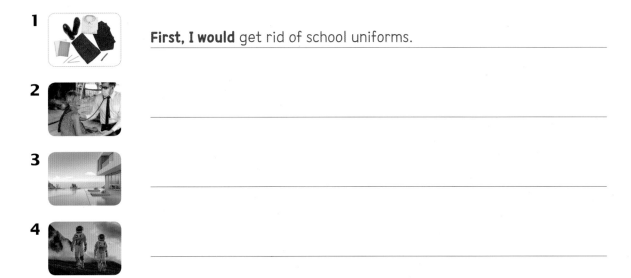

1 **First, I would** get rid of school uniforms.

2 _____

3 _____

4 _____

C Look at the example and rewrite the sentences.

I get rid of school uniforms. Students are happier.
→ **If** I **got** rid of school uniforms, students **would be** happier.

💡 When the *if*-clause is the past simple, use "would/could/might" in the main clause.

1 I write a popular children's series. Children want to read more.

→ _____

2 I visit the moon. Many people become interested in space.

→ _____

3 I find a cure for cancer. Many patients may not die.

→ _____

4 I buy my own private airplane. I can travel around the world.

→ _____

D Look at the pictures. Write the sentences with the words in the box.

| astronaut | writer | ~~principal~~ | doctor |

💡 Use the preposition "as" to refer to the role of a person.

1   (make those changes at once)

As a principal, I would make those changes at once.

2 (act that way)

_____

3 (write those books)

_____

4 (do those activities)

_____

56

E **Read the short paragraph. Correct the mistakes and rewrite the paragraph.**

I want to be the CEO of a large company. If I <u>am</u> a CEO, I would take two actions to improve my company. First, I would <u>improving</u> the quality of my company's products. If I did that, customers <u>will</u> enjoy using my products more.

_____

_____

_____

_____

Writing Skills

To list two points in an essay, you can use the following words:

· *First, ~ / Second, ~*   · *The first ~ is that... / The second ~ is that...*

Example First, / The first thing is that I would get rid of school uniforms. Second, / The second thing is that I would change the times school starts and ends.

Rewrite the sentences by using the words in parentheses.

1 I would treat the poor for free. I would try to find a cure for cancer. (first / second)

→ _____

2 I would travel in space. I would talk to people about space.
(the first thing is that / the second thing is that)

→ _____

_____

Brainstorming

Brainstorm your ideas about what you would like to be and what you would do if you were that person.

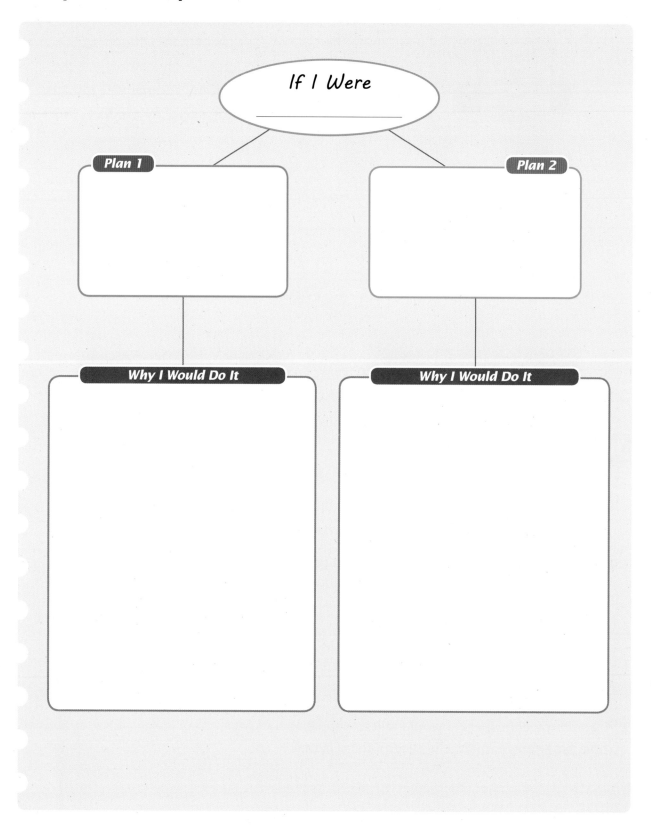

If I Were
_____

Plan 1

Plan 2

Why I Would Do It

Why I Would Do It

Outlining

Based on your brainstorming, complete the outline of your essay.

Title	
Introduction	
Body	**Plan 1**
	Plan 2
Conclusion	

Unit 6
Taking Online Classes

Writing Goal	To write about my preference between two choices
Type of Writing	Persuasive Essay
	A persuasive essay encourages a reader to make a choice by providing evidence and examples.

Before You Write

A **Read and answer the questions.**

1 Do you prefer to take online classes or to take traditional classes at a school?

2 What is your experience with that type of class?

3 How did you benefit from taking that type of class?

B **Fill in the chart with the phrases in the box.**

take online classes	I can travel somewhere far away
read paper books	I can study from my bedroom
take a long vacation	they are comfortable for the eyes

I prefer to...	because...
• _____	• _____
• _____	• _____
• _____	• _____

Analyzing the Model Essay

A **Read the model essay and answer the questions.**

The Advantages of Online Classes

Many people prefer to attend classes at schools. I do not though. While traditional classes have some benefits, they are not the best way to learn. Instead, online classes are better.

I took an online math class in summer. I learned more in that class than I did in any other school class. In the online class, there were no noisy students or other problems. So the teacher could just focus on teaching the class.

Moreover, online classes are much more convenient than traditional classes. I do not like to wake up early to go to school. Thanks to online classes, I can study from my bedroom.

Students learn more in online classes. They find the classes more convenient, too. This makes them far superior to traditional classes.

1 What is the essay about?

_____

2 What does the writer think about the online math class he took in summer?

_____

3 Why does the writer think online classes are convenient?

_____

B **Read the model essay again and complete the brainstorming and outlining.**

The Advantages of Online Classes

Advantage 1

_____
in an online math class

- _____ or other problems
- the teacher could focus on teaching the class

Advantage 2

much more _____

- do not like to wake up early to go to school
- can study _____

Title _____	
Introduction	• many people prefer to _____ • my preference: _____ are better
Body	**Advantage 1** _____ in summer → learned more than I did in any other school class • there were _____ or other problems • the teacher could just _____ **Advantage 2** are _____ than traditional classes • do not like to _____ • can _____
Conclusion	• students _____ and find the classes more convenient • far _____ traditional classes

Collecting Ideas

Look at the example. Fill in the blanks with the phrases in the box.

students can ask questions easily	~~can study from my bedroom~~
are more comfortable for the eyes	can store hundreds of books
can visit various places in different seasons	can travel somewhere far away

1

- Online classes
- no noisy students or other problems
- _can study from my bedroom_

2

- Traditional classes
- _____
- can socialize and learn with students in person

3

- E-books
- can save trees
- _____
  on a single device

4

- Paper books
- _____
- don't need electric power or batteries

5

- A long vacation
- _____
- can do many activities

6

- Several short vacations
- will not forget what I have learned
- _____

Sentence Practice

A **Look at the pictures. Write the sentences with the phrases in the box.**

read e-books	~~attend classes at schools~~
study in groups	have several short vacations

1 **Many people prefer to** attend classes at schools.

2 _____

3 _____

4 _____

B **Look at the example and rewrite the sentences.**

Traditional classes have some benefits. They are not the best way to learn.
→ **While** traditional classes have some benefits, they are not the best way to learn.

💡 You can use "while" to give an opinion different from someone else's. It means "although."

1 E-books are becoming popular. I still prefer paper books.

→ _____

2 A long vacation sounds nice. It can be boring.

→ _____

3 Studying in a group can be helpful. It is not for everyone.

→ _____

4 Studying abroad has its advantages. It also has its disadvantages.

→ _____

C Look at the example and write the sentences.

💡 Use "much/even/far/a lot" to emphasize a comparative.

1 (online classes / much / convenient / traditional classes)

→ Online classes **are much more convenient than** traditional classes.

2 (e-books / a lot / good / paper books)

→ _____

3 (several short vacations / even / exciting / a long vacation)

→ _____

4 (studying alone / far / effective / studying in a group)

→ _____

Your Idea

5 _____

D Look at the example and write the sentences.

1 online classes / study from my bedroom

→ **Thanks to** online classes, **I can** study from my bedroom.

2 e-books / store hundreds of books on a single device

→ _____

3 having a long vacation / do many activities

→ _____

4 studying in a group / strengthen my knowledge by teaching others

→ _____

Your Idea

5 _____

E **Read the short paragraph. Correct the mistakes and rewrite the paragraph.**

Many people prefer to study in groups. I do not though. When studying in a group can be helpful, it is not for everyone. When I study alone, I can learn at my own pace. Moreover, studying alone is very more effective than studying in a group. Thanks to study alone, I can focus on what I need to study.

_____

_____

_____

_____

Writing Skills

When you want to give more information, you can use the following words:

· *Moreover,*   · *In addition,*

Example In online classes, there are no noisy students or other problems. Moreover, / In addition, online classes are much more convenient than traditional classes.

Rewrite the sentences by using the words in parentheses.

1 E-books can save trees. I can store hundreds of books on a single device. (moreover)

→ _____

2 During a long vacation, I can travel somewhere far away. I can do many activities. (in addition)

→ _____

Brainstorming

Brainstorm your ideas about your preference between two choices.

(e.g. online classes vs. traditional classes, e-books vs. paper books, a long vacation vs. several short vacations)

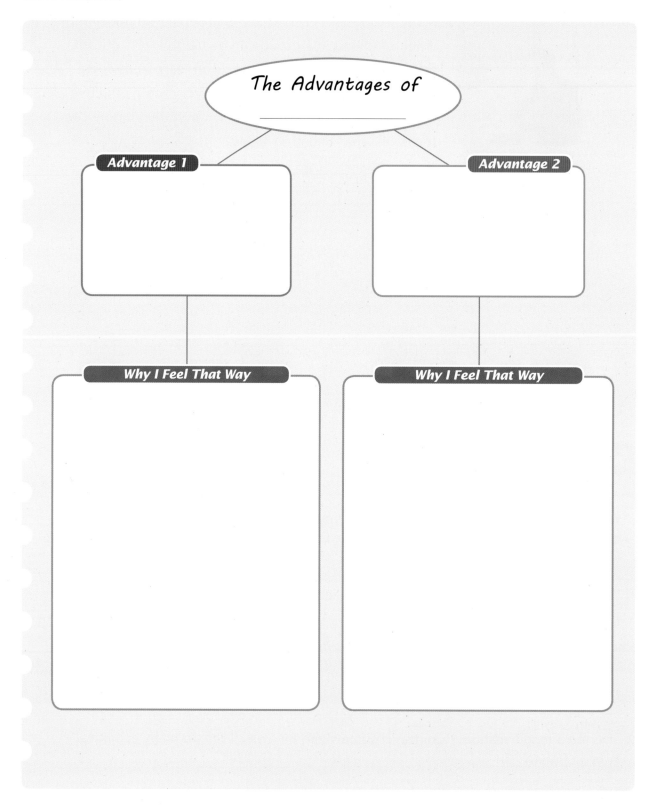

The Advantages of
_____

Advantage 1

Advantage 2

Why I Feel That Way

Why I Feel That Way

Outlining

Based on your brainstorming, complete the outline of your essay.

Title	
Introduction	
Body	**Advantage 1** **Advantage 2**
Conclusion	

Unit 7

The Environment

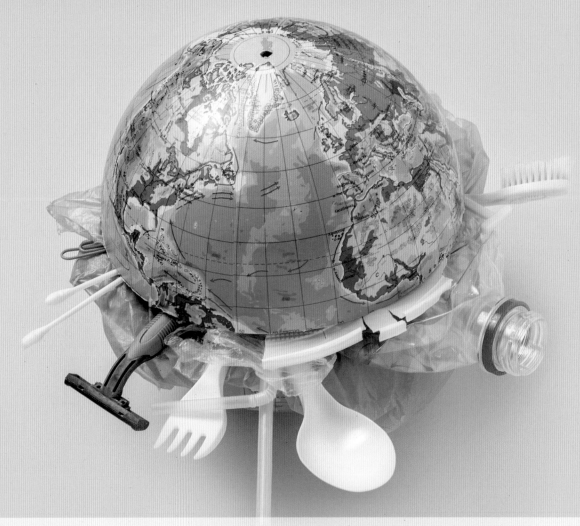

Writing Goal	To write about human activities and how they affect the environment
Type of Writing	Expository Essay
	An expository essay gives information about a topic or explains how to do something.

Before You Write

A **Read and answer the questions.**

1 Do you think the environment is in danger?

2 What are some human activities that affect the environment?

3 What are some impacts of these activities on the environment?

B **Match the pictures with the correct phrases in the box.**

use plastic products	burn fossil fuels	cut down trees
eat meat	put pesticides into the soil	drive cars

1

2

3

4

5

6

Analyzing the Model Essay

Ⓐ Read the model essay and answer the questions.

Environmental Problems

These days, there are all kinds of environmental problems. Regular people are often causing them.

It seems that people know they should take care of the Earth, but they are not doing that. For instance, more and more people are using plastic products these days. These items do not break down quickly. Instead, they get into rivers and oceans. As a result, rivers and oceans have been filled with plastic waste. Many fish and other marine life are also dying because of this garbage.

People put pesticides into the soil to grow crops as well. These poisons are polluting the ground. Due to them, no plants can grow in some places. Pesticides are making the water supply unsafe to drink, too.

In conclusion, plastics and pesticides are two major causes of pollution. They are killing plants and animals. They are also reducing the quality of the land and the water.

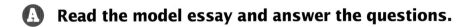

1 What are two ways that people are harming the environment?

1) _____

2) _____

2 How is plastic waste affecting the environment?

_____

3 How are pesticides affecting the environment?

_____

B **Read the model essay again and complete the brainstorming and outlining.**

Environmental Problems

Human Activity 1

use _____

- rivers and oceans have been filled with
  _____
- _____ are dying

Human Activity 2

put _____ into the soil

- plants can't grow
- make _____ unsafe to drink

Title	_____
Introduction	• these days, there are all kinds of environmental problems • _____ are often causing them
Body	**Human Activity 1** people are _____ • don't _____ and get into rivers and oceans → rivers and oceans _____ • fish and other marine life _____ **Human Activity 2** people _____ to grow crops • are polluting the ground → _____ in some places • are making _____
Conclusion	• _____ and _____ : two major causes of pollution • are killing _____ and reducing the quality of _____

Collecting Ideas

Look at the example. Fill in the blanks with the phrases in the box.

> ~~fish and other marine life are dying~~
> make the water supply unsafe to drink
> cows produce greenhouse gases
>
> the Earth's climate is changing
> there are fewer trees on the Earth
> people have a hard time breathing

1

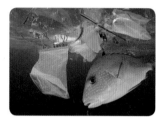

- use plastic products
- fill rivers and oceans with plastic waste
- fish and other marine life are dying

2

- put pesticides into the soil
- no plants grow in some places
- _____

3

- drive their own cars
- pollute the air
- _____

4

- cut down trees
- _____
- make animals lose their homes

5

- eat meat
- destroy rainforests to raise cows
- _____

6

- burn fossil fuels
- _____
- cause acid rain

74

Sentence Practice

A **Look at the pictures and complete the sentences.**

💡 Use "it seems that ~" to give your opinion.

1

It seems that people know they should take care of the Earth ,
but they are not doing that. (take care of the Earth)

2

_____ ,
but they are still doing it. (not / pollute)

3

_____ ,
but they are not doing that. (save energy)

4

_____ ,
but they are still doing it. (not / waste food)

B **Look at the pictures. Write the sentences with the phrases in the box.**

are using electronic items	are buying things online
~~are using plastic products~~	do not take buses or subways

1

More and more people are using plastic products **these days**.

2

_____

3

_____

4

_____

5 Your Idea

_____

C Look at the example and rewrite the sentences.

💡 Form the present perfect passive by using "have/has been + p.p."

1 People have filled <u>rivers and oceans</u> with plastic waste.

→ Rivers and oceans **have been filled** with plastic waste.

2 People have polluted <u>the air</u> with smoke.

→ _____

3 People have destroyed <u>nearly half of the world's rainforests</u>.

→ _____

D Look at the example and write the sentences.

1 (put pesticides into the soil / grow crops)

→ **People** put pesticides into the soil **to** grow crops **as well**.

2 (cut down trees / make paper and furniture)

→ _____

3 (burn fossil fuels / create energy)

→ _____

E Look at the pictures. Complete the sentences with the phrases in the box.

| ~~grow in some places~~   is changing   there are fewer trees |

1 Due to them, no plants can _____ grow in some places _____ .

2 Due to them, _____ on the Earth.

3 Due to them, the Earth's climate _____ .

F Read the short paragraph. Correct the mistakes and rewrite the paragraph.

It seems to people know they should protect the environment, but they are not doing that. For instance, many and many people are eating meat for every meal these days. To raise cows, farmers want more land. As a result, nearly half of the rainforests have destroyed.

↓

_____

_____

_____

_____

Writing Skills

When you begin your concluding paragraph, you can start by writing:

· In conclusion,   · To conclude,

Example In conclusion, / To conclude, plastics and pesticides are two major causes of pollution.

Rewrite the sentences by using the words in parentheses.

1 Cars and deforestation are two major causes of environmental problems. (in conclusion)

→ _____

2 Eating meat and excessive energy use harm the environment and cause global warming. (to conclude)

→ _____

Brainstorming

Brainstorm your idea about environmental problems.

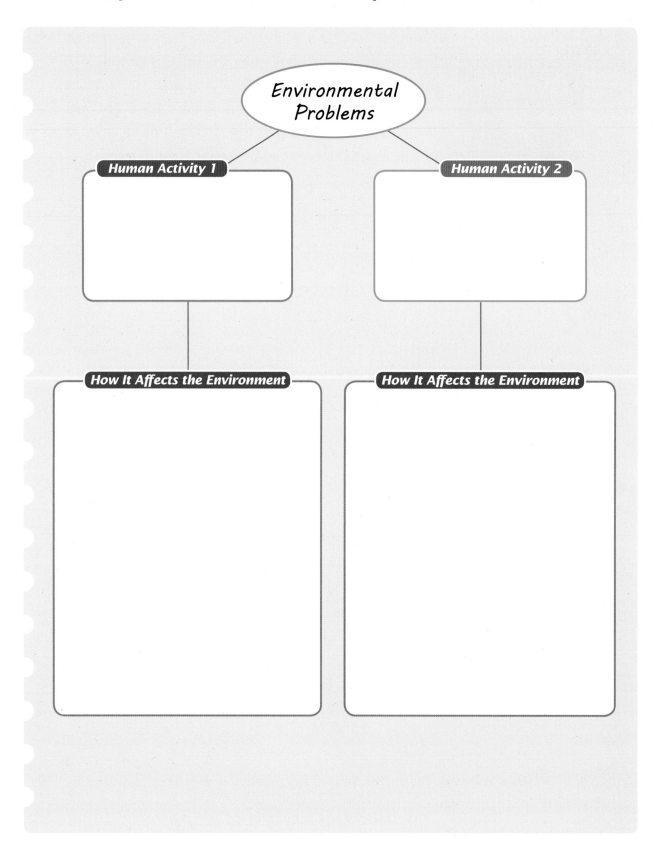

Outlining

Based on your brainstorming, complete the outline of your essay.

Title	
Introduction	
Body	**Human Activity 1**
	Human Activity 2
Conclusion	

Unit 8

Mobile Phones at Schools

Writing Goal	To write about whether I agree or disagree with a statement
Type of Writing	Persuasive Essay
	A persuasive essay encourages a reader to make a choice by providing evidence and examples.

Before You Write

A Read and answer the questions.

1 Do you believe that students should have mobile phones at schools?

2 How could having mobile phones at schools benefit students?

3 How could having mobile phones at schools harm students?

B Fill in the chart with the phrases in the box.

| class discussions | part-time jobs | ban mobile phones | proud of |
| school uniforms | responsibility | learn the material | in class |

I believe that...	because...
• school should _____	• students use their phones _____
• teachers should have more _____	• students _____ better
• students should wear _____	• they make students _____ their schools
• teens should have _____	• teens can learn _____

Analyzing the Model Essay

A   **Read the model essay and answer the questions.**

Using Mobile Phones at Schools

I have a mobile phone and use it a lot. But I do not agree that students should use mobile phones at schools. In fact, I believe that schools should ban mobile phones.

So many students seem like they cannot live without their phones. They even use their phones in class. Students not only send text messages on their phones but also play games on them. The more they use their phones, the worse their grades are.

When students use their mobile phones in class, they cause problems for others. For example, I cannot focus on my lessons at times. I go to school to learn. I do not want students distracting me with their phones.

Schools need to ban mobile phones at once. They make students do poorly in class. And they bother other students.

1   What is the writer's opinion about using mobile phones at schools?

_____

2   How does the writer say mobile phones affect students' grades?

_____

3   What problem does the writer have because of students using mobile phones in class?

_____

B **Read the model essay again and complete the brainstorming and outlining.**

Using Mobile Phones at Schools

Reason 1

_____
in class

- _____ and play games
- the more they use their phones
  → _____

Reason 2

_____
for others

- cannot _____
- do not want students distracting me

	Title _____
Introduction	• do not agree that students should use mobile phones at schools • believe that _____
Body	**Reason 1** students _____ • not only send text messages but also _____ • the more _____, the worse _____ **Reason 2** students _____ • I cannot _____ at times • I go to school to learn → do not want students _____
Conclusion	• schools need to ban mobile phones at once • they make students _____ and _____

Collecting Ideas

Look at the example. Fill in the blanks with the phrases in the box.

learn the material better	can learn responsibility
~~use their phones in class~~	takes away from leisure time
can play sports on weekends	make students proud of their schools

1

- Schools should ban mobile phones.
- _use their phones in class_
- cause problems for others

2

- Teachers should have more class discussions.
- can improve their speaking skills
- _____

3

- Students should wear school uniforms.
- do not have to focus on fashion
- _____

4

- Teens should not play sports after school.
- need to study more instead
- _____

5

- Students should not have daily homework.
- _____
- is not always effective

6

- Teens should have part-time jobs.
- _____
- can learn how to manage money

Sentence Practice

A **Look at the pictures and complete the sentences.**

1. (schools / ban mobile phones)

   In fact, _____**I believe that** schools **should** ban mobile phones_____ .

2. (teens / have part-time jobs)

   In fact, _____ .

3. (students / wear school uniforms)

   In fact, _____ .

4. (teachers / have more class discussions)

   In fact, _____ .

5. Your Idea _____

B **Look at the example and rewrite the sentences.**

💡 Combine two similar points by using "not only A but also B."

1. Students send text messages on their phones. They also play games on them.

   → Students **not only** send text messages on their phones **but also** play games on them.

2. Teens waste time playing sports. They also do not study enough.

   → _____

3. Teens get valuable work experience. They also learn how to deal with people.

   → _____

4. Class discussions let students learn to speak better. They also make them more confident.

   → _____

C **Look at the example and complete the sentences.**

💡 "The + comparative, the + comparative" shows how one thing depends upon another thing.

1 As they use their phones more, their grades are worse.

→ The _____ **more** they use their phones _____, the _____ **worse** their grades are _____.

2 As they talk in class more, their speaking skills get better.

→ The _____, the _____.

3 As they do more homework every day, they have more stress.

→ The _____, the _____.

4 As they play sports more, they become more tired at night.

→ The _____, the _____.

5 Your Idea

_____

D **Look at the pictures. Complete the sentences with the phrases in the box.**

~~cause problems for others~~	do not have to focus on fashion
can learn the material better	can learn to manage money

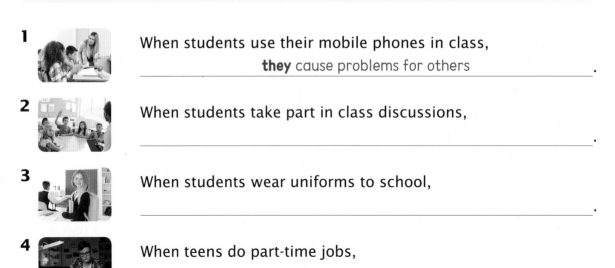

1 When students use their mobile phones in class,

_____ **they** cause problems for others _____.

2 When students take part in class discussions,

_____.

3 When students wear uniforms to school,

_____.

4 When teens do part-time jobs,

_____.

86

E **Read the short paragraph. Correct the mistakes and rewrite the paragraph.**

I believe <u>what</u> teens should not play sports after school. Teens not only waste time playing sports <u>and</u> do not study enough. The more they play sports, <u>the low</u> their grades become. When students play sports after school, they become too tired to do homework at night.

↓

_____

_____

_____

_____

Writing Skills

When you agree or disagree with a statement, you can use:
- *I agree that ~*   - *I do not agree that ~ / I disagree that ~*

Example I agree that students should be able to use mobile phones at schools.
I do not agree that / I disagree that students should be able to use mobile phones at schools.

Rewrite the sentences by using the words in parentheses.

1 Students should wear school uniforms. (agree)

   ➡ _____

2 Students should have daily homework. (disagree)

   ➡ _____

Brainstorming

Brainstorm your ideas about a topic that you agree or disagree with.
Refer to the topics in Collecting Ideas.

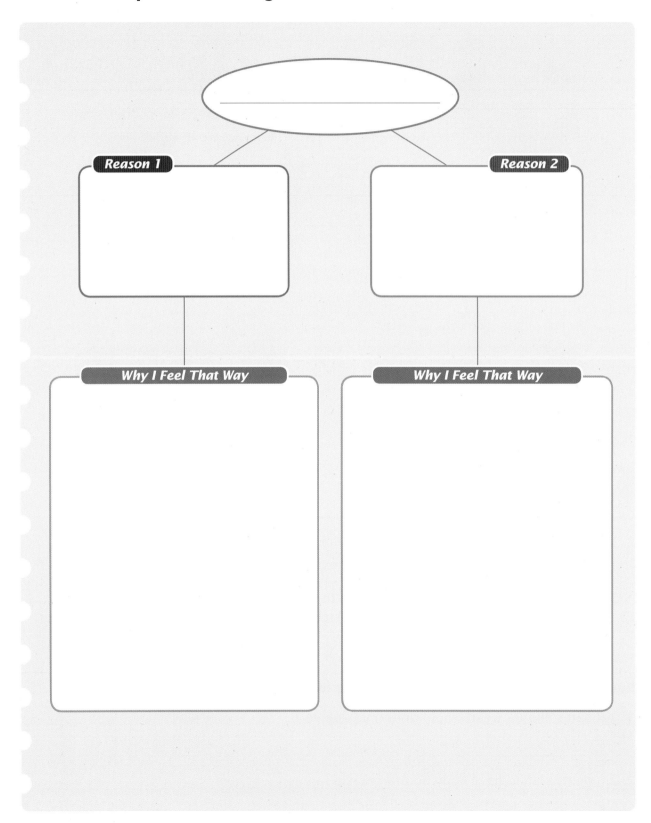

Reason 1

Reason 2

Why I Feel That Way

Why I Feel That Way

Outlining

Based on your brainstorming, complete the outline of your essay.

Title	
Introduction	
Body	**Reason 1**
	Reason 2
Conclusion	

Vocabulary & Structure Review

Unit 1
My Future

Read the words and phrases. Write the meaning next to each word and phrase.

1	item		11	star (*v.*)	
2	coral reef		12	perform	
3	tropical fish		13	orchestra	
4	the Northern Lights		14	snow-covered	
5	fascinated		15	decide to	
6	the Arctic Circle		16	be interested in	
7	amazing		17	go scuba diving	
8	though (*ad.*)		18	so far	
9	national park		19	go on a safari	
10	president		20	a dream come true	

1 the relative pronoun "what" = the thing which

e.g <u>What</u> I am interested in is scuba diving.

2 to-infinitive as a subject complement

e.g Another one of my dreams is <u>to see</u> the Northern Lights.

Unit 2
My Favorite Website

Words & Phrases

Read the words and phrases. Write the meaning next to each word and phrase.

1	education (*a.* educational)		11	share (*v.*)	
2	article		12	ship (*v.*)	
3	various		13	latest (*a.*)	
4	topic		14	book review	
5	history		15	all the time	
6	geography		16	focus on	
7	reason		17	in my opinion	
8	improve		18	check out	
9	verbal (*a.*)		19	search for	
10	post (*v.*) (= upload)		20	stay updated	

Structures

1   present participle (verb-ing) as an adjective

e.g Ducksters is a website <u>focusing</u> on education.

2   present perfect continuous: have/has been + verb-ing

e.g I <u>have been visiting</u> Ducksters for many years.

Unit 3
My Most Memorable Trip

Read the words and phrases. Write the meaning next to each word and phrase.

1	memorable		11	souvenir	
2	fly (v.)		12	painting	
3	capital (n.)		13	tour (v.)	
4	ancient (a.)		14	traditional	
5	empire		15	monument	
6	cathedral		16	take place	
7	chapel		17	drop by	
8	ride (ride-rode-ridden)		18	take a photo	
9	return (v.)		19	go on a cruise	
10	cherry blossom		20	in person	

Structures

1 the relative adverb "where"

　e.g　Italy is a country <u>where</u> lots of history took place.

2 past perfect: had + p.p.

　e.g　I <u>had</u> never <u>ridden</u> in a gondola before.

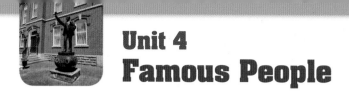

Unit 4
Famous People

Read the words and phrases. Write the meaning next to each word and phrase.

1	inventor		11	characteristic	
2	success		12	author (= writer)	
3	positive		13	educator	
4	fail (↔ succeed)		14	practice	
5	quit (v.)		15	inspire	
6	hardworking		16	sculpture	
7	lifetime		17	publish	
8	phonograph		18	despite	
9	record (v.)		19	give up	
10	motion picture camera		20	without a doubt (= without question)	

Structures

1 nonrestrictive adjective clauses: "~, which"

e.g One was the phonograph, <u>which</u> let people record sounds.
Another was the motion picture camera, <u>which</u> people used to make movies.

2 whenever + subject + verb

e.g <u>Whenever</u> you think of inventors, you should think of Thomas Edison.

Unit 5
If I Were...

Read the words and phrases. Write the meaning next to each word and phrase.

1	principal (*n.*)		11	product	
2	school uniform		12	private	
3	complain		13	get rid of	
4	dislike (← like)		14	have trouble verb-ing	
5	clothes		15	fall asleep	
6	popular		16	pay attention	
7	treat (*v.*)		17	wide awake	
8	cure (*n.*)		18	at once	
9	cancer		19	travel in space	
10	quality		20	for free	

Structures

1 If + subject + were/past simple, subject + would/could/might + verb

e.g If I were a principal, I would make two big changes to help the students.

If I found a cure for cancer, many patients might not die.

2 the preposition "as"

e.g As a principal, I would make those changes at once.

Unit 6
Taking Online Classes

Words & Phrases

Read the words and phrases. Write the meaning next to each word and phrase.

1	advantage (↔ disadvantage)		11	device	
2	prefer		12	comfortable	
3	attend		13	vacation	
4	benefit (*n.*)		14	activity	
5	noisy		15	season	
6	moreover (= in addition)		16	effective	
7	convenient		17	thanks to	
8	socialize		18	superior to	
9	store (*v.*)		19	electric power	
10	single (*a.*)		20	far away	

Structures

1 while + subject + verb (= although)

e.g <u>While</u> traditional classes have some benefits, they are not the best way to learn.

2 much/even/far/a lot + comparative

e.g Online classes are <u>much more convenient</u> than traditional classes.
This makes them <u>far superior</u> to traditional classes.

Unit 7
The Environment

Read the words and phrases. Write the meaning next to each word and phrase.

1	environmental (*n.* environment)		11	unsafe	
2	regular		12	breathe	
3	cause (*v., n.*)		13	destroy	
4	marine (*a.*)		14	rainforest	
5	garbage (= waste)		15	climate	
6	pesticide		16	fossil fuel	
7	crop (*n.*)		17	take care of	
8	poison (*n.*)		18	break down	
9	pollute		19	be filled with	
10	water supply		20	due to (= because of)	

Structures

1 It seems that + subject + verb

e.g It seems that people know they should take care of the Earth, but they are not doing that.

2 present perfect passive: have/has been + p.p.

e.g As a result, rivers and oceans have been filled with plastic waste.

Unit 8
Mobile Phones at Schools

Words & Phrases

Read the words and phrases. Write the meaning next to each word and phrase.

1	mobile phone (= cellphone)		11	proud	
2	agree (↔ disagree)		12	teen (= teenager)	
3	ban (v.)		13	daily	
4	text message		14	leisure time	
5	grade (n.)		15	responsibility	
6	distract		16	manage (v.)	
7	poorly (ad.)		17	part-time job	
8	bother (v.)		18	at times (= sometimes)	
9	discussion		19	proud of	
10	material		20	take away from	

Structures

1 not only A but also B

e.g Students <u>not only</u> send text messages on their phones <u>but also</u> play games on them.

2 the + comparative, the + comparative

e.g <u>The more</u> they use their phones, <u>the worse</u> their grades are.

Memo

Memo

Memo

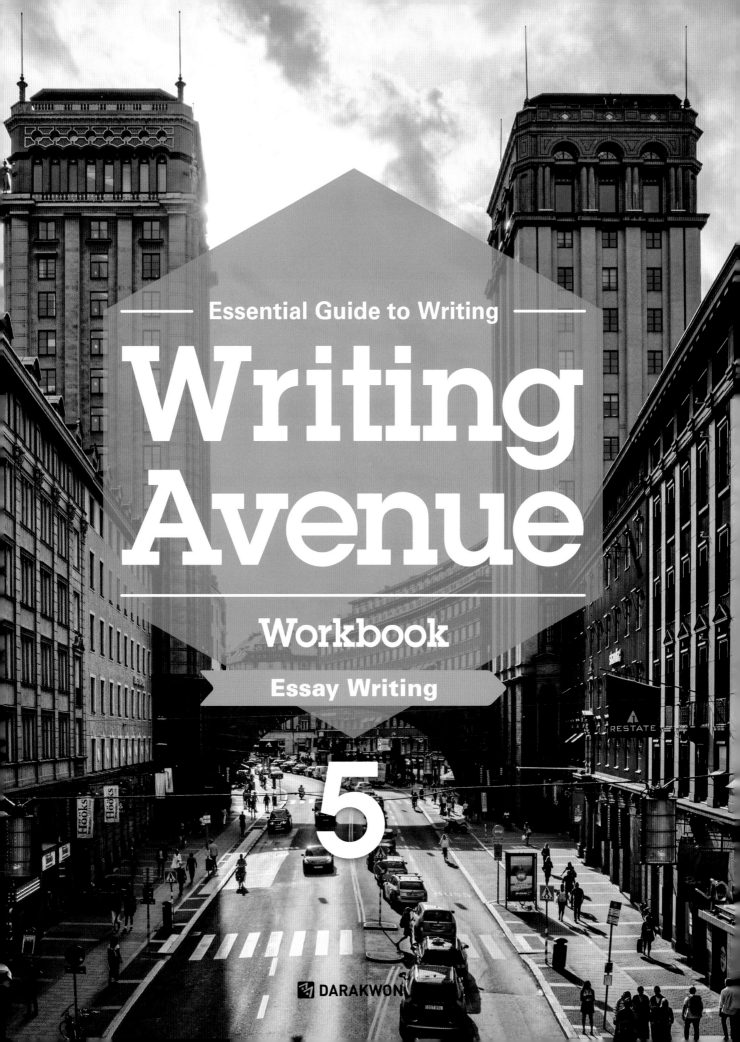

Essential Guide to Writing

Writing Avenue

Workbook

Essay Writing

5

DARAKWON

Essential Guide to Writing

Writing Avenue

Workbook

Essay Writing

5

DARAKWON

Unit 1 My Future

Ⓐ Look at the example and rewrite the sentences.

1 I am interested in scuba diving.

→ **What** I am interested in **is** scuba diving.

2 I am interested in animals.

→ _____

3 I am interested in mountain climbing.

→ _____

4 I am interested in music.

→ _____

Ⓑ Look at the example and write the sentences.

become a writer	play the violin
~~see the Northern Lights~~	make movies

1 **Another one of my dreams is to see** the Northern Lights.

2 _____

3 _____

4 _____

2

C **Write the correct number in each blank. Then, write the sentences.**

1	A bucket list is a list of things	_____	a shark
2	As a result, I decided	_____	in the Caribbean Sea
3	I would love to go scuba diving	_____	thinking of others though
4	It has many beautiful coral reefs, so	_____	to make my own bucket list
5	I might even see	_____	a person wants to do before dying
6	I became fascinated by them	_____	I could see all kinds of tropical fish
7	I think seeing them	_____	from the Arctic Circle would be amazing
8	I will keep	_____	when I saw them on a TV program last year

1 _____

2 _____

3 _____

4 _____

5 _____

6 _____

7 _____

8 _____

First Draft

Write the first draft by using the outline. Then, revise and edit your essay.

Title	
Introduction	
Body	
Conclusion	

Revising Checklist

1. Did you explain why you thought about making a bucket list in the introduction? ☐
2. Did you write two items on your bucket list and their details? ☐
3. Did you use the relative pronoun "what" and a to-infinitive as a subject complement? ☐

Editing Checklist   Capitalization ☐   Punctuation ☐   Grammar ☐   Spelling ☐

Final Draft

Write the final draft.

Title	

Unit 2 My Favorite Website

A Look at the pictures. Complete the sentences with the words and phrases in the box.

| ~~education~~ | sharing videos | online shopping | online searches |

1 Ducksters is ___**a website focusing on** education___.

2 Google is ___.

3 YouTube is ___.

4 Amazon.com is ___.

B Look at the example and rewrite the sentences.

1 I visit Ducksters. (for many years)

→ I **have been visiting** Ducksters for many years. ___

2 I use Amazon.com. (for a long time)

→ ___

3 I make videos for YouTube. (since 2019)

→ ___

4 I post on Instagram. (for two years)

→ ___

6

C Write the correct number in each blank. Then, write the sentences.

1	I use the Internet all the time,	_____	to learn new things there
2	The website that I like more than	_____	verbal skills while I also have fun
3	So it has articles	_____	of the best websites on the Internet
4	I love to read the articles and	_____	that it has lots of games
5	Another reason that I like Ducksters is	_____	on various topics
6	So I can improve my math and	_____	any others is called Ducksters
7	In my opinion, Ducksters is one	_____	should check out the website
8	If you want to learn and have fun, you	_____	so I visit many websites

1 _____

2 _____

3 _____

4 _____

5 _____

6 _____

7 _____

8 _____

First Draft

Write the first draft by using the outline. Then, revise and edit your essay.

Title	
Introduction	
Body	
Conclusion	

Revising Checklist

1. Did you provide the name of your favorite website in the introduction? ☐
2. Did you write two reasons the website is your favorite and their details? ☐
3. Did you use a present participle (verb-ing) phrase that modifies a noun and "have/has been + verb-ing"? ☐

Editing Checklist   Capitalization ☐   Punctuation ☐   Grammar ☐   Spelling ☐

Final Draft

Write the final draft.

Title _____

Unit 3 My Most Memorable Trip

(A) **Look at the example and write the sentences.**

1 (Italy / a country / lots of history took place)

→ Italy **is** a country **where** lots of history took place.

2 (Korea / a country / you can enjoy four seasons)

→ _____

3 (Hawaii / a place / many people spend their vacations)

→ _____

4 (India / a country / there are many traditions and a lot of culture)

→ _____

(B) **Look at the pictures. Write the sentences with the phrases in the box.**

see such a beautiful sunset	~~ride in a gondola~~
eat traditional Indian food	climb to the top of a mountain

1 **I had never ridden** in a gondola **before.**

2 _____

3 _____

4 _____

10

C **Write the correct number in each blank. Then, write the sentences.**

1	Last summer, I traveled to Italy	_____	one of my favorite cities
2	It was my first trip to Italy, so	_____	I was very excited
3	It was the capital of	_____	with my family
4	There, we saw St. Peter's Cathedral and the Sistine Chapel	_____	the ancient Roman Empire
5	Next, we went to Venice,	_____	because we saw lots of beautiful places
6	We dropped	_____	by St. Mark's Basilica and the Palazzo Ducale
7	I will never forget the wonderful trip we had	_____	return one day since the cities were so wonderful
8	I would also love to	_____	as well as some art museums

1 _____

2 _____

3 _____

4 _____

5 _____

6 _____

7 _____

8 _____

First Draft

Write the first draft by using the outline. Then, revise and edit your essay.

Title	_____
Introduction	
Body	
Conclusion	

Revising Checklist

1. Did you explain where you went on your most memorable trip in the introduction? ☐
2. Did you write the places that you visited and their details? ☐
3. Did you use the relative adverb "where" and "had + p.p."? ☐

Editing Checklist   Capitalization ☐   Punctuation ☐   Grammar ☐   Spelling ☐

Final Draft

Write the final draft.

Title _____

Unit 4 Famous People

A **Look at the example and write the sentences.**

1 One was the phonograph. It let people record sounds.

→ One was the phonograph, **which** let people record sounds.

2 One was the MVP award. It showed he was the best player.

→ _____

3 One was *David*. It is a sculpture.

→ _____

4 One was *Ace Ventura: Pet Detective*. It made audiences laugh a lot.

→ _____

B **Look at the pictures. Write the sentences with the words in the boxes.**

| artists   authors and educators |
| basketball players   ~~inventors~~ |

| Michael Jordan   ~~Thomas Edison~~ |
| Jim Carrey   Helen Keller |

1

Whenever you think of inventors, **you should think of** Thomas Edison.

2

_____

3

_____

4

_____

14

C **Write the correct number in each blank. Then, write the sentences.**

1 Thomas Edison was one of

2 Edison did poorly at school, but he was

3 For instance, when he was trying

4 He was also a very

5 Edison enjoyed

6 Because Edison never stopped trying, people

7 During Edison's lifetime, he invented

8 Without a doubt, two characteristics made him

____ hardworking man

____ the world's greatest inventors

____ more than 1,000 items

____ working all the time

____ always positive and never gave up

____ around the world can enjoy indoor lighting

____ a great inventor and famous man

____ to invent the light bulb, he failed 10,000 times

1 _____

2 _____

3 _____

4 _____

5 _____

6 _____

7 _____

8 _____

First Draft

Write the first draft by using the outline. Then, revise and edit your essay.

Title	
Introduction	
Body	
Conclusion	

1. Did you explain who the person is in the introduction? ☐
2. Did you write two characteristics of the person and their details? ☐
3. Did you use a relative clause with a comma and "whenever"? ☐

Editing Checklist   Capitalization ☐   Punctuation ☐   Grammar ☐   Spelling ☐

Final Draft

Write the final draft.

Title	

Unit 5 If I Were...

A **Look at the example and complete the sentences.**

1 (get rid of / be happier)

→ If I ___got rid of___ school uniforms, students ___**would** be happier___ .

2 (do / enjoy using my products)

→ If I _____ that, customers _____ .

3 (find / may live longer)

→ If I _____ a cure for cancer, many patients _____ .

4 (buy / can travel around the world)

→ If I _____ my own private airplane, I _____ .

B **Look at the example and write the sentences.**

1 | a principal / make those changes at once |

→ **As** a principal, **I would** make those changes at once. _____

2 | a CEO / take those actions |

→ _____

3 | a doctor / do those activities |

→ _____

4 | a writer / write those books |

→ _____

18

C **Write the correct number in each blank. Then, write the sentences.**

1 If I were a principal, I would make

2 First, I would get

3 Many students complain

4 They would rather

5 Second, I would change the times

6 Most students have trouble waking up,

7 Others have a hard time

8 Then, the students would be

_____ paying attention

_____ wear other clothes

_____ wide awake all day long

_____ rid of school uniforms

_____ so they often fall asleep during class

_____ two big changes to help the students

_____ school starts and ends

_____ about their uniforms and dislike wearing them

1 _____

2 _____

3 _____

4 _____

5 _____

6 _____

7 _____

8 _____

First Draft

Write the first draft by using the outline. Then, revise and edit your essay.

Title	
Introduction	
Body	
Conclusion	

1. Did you explain why you want to become that person in the future in the introduction? ☐
2. Did you write two activities you would do as that person? ☐
3. Did you use "If + subject + were/past simple, subject + would + verb" and the preposition "as"? ☐

Editing Checklist   Capitalization ☐   Punctuation ☐   Grammar ☐   Spelling ☐

20

Final Draft

Write the final draft.

Title _____

Unit 6 Taking Online Classes

A Look at the example and combine the sentences in the boxes.

1. ~~Traditional classes have some benefits.~~
2. E-books are becoming popular.
3. A long vacation sounds nice.
4. Studying abroad has its advantage.

It can be boring.
It also has its disadvantages.
~~They are not the best way to learn.~~
I still like paper books better.

1 **While** traditional classes have some benefits, they are not the best way to learn

2 _____

3 _____

4 _____

B Look at the example and complete the sentences.

1 (much / convenient)

→ Online classes are ____ much **more** convenient **than** ____ traditional classes.

2 (far / good)

→ E-books are _____ paper books.

3 (even / exciting)

→ A long vacation is _____ several short vacations.

4 (a lot / effective)

→ Studying alone is _____ studying in a group.

C **Write the correct number in each blank. Then, write the sentences.**

1 Many people prefer _____ focus on teaching the class

2 I learned more in that class _____ to attend classes at schools

3 In the online class, there were _____ I can study from my bedroom

4 So the teacher could just _____ more convenient, too

5 I do not like to _____ superior to traditional classes

6 Thanks to online classes, _____ no noisy students or other problems

7 They find the classes _____ wake up early to go to school

8 This makes them far _____ than I did in any other school class

1 _____

2 _____

3 _____

4 _____

5 _____

6 _____

7 _____

8 _____

First Draft

Write the first draft by using the outline. Then, revise and edit your essay.

Title	
Introduction	
Body	
Conclusion	

Revising Checklist

1. Did you explain which choice you prefer in the introduction? ☐
2. Did you write two reasons that you like that choice and their details? ☐
3. Did you use "while" to mean "although" and "much/even/far/a lot + comparative"? ☐

Editing Checklist   Capitalization ☐   Punctuation ☐   Grammar ☐   Spelling ☐

Final Draft

Write the final draft.

Title	_____

Unit 7 The Environment

A **Look at the example and complete the sentences.**

1 People know they should take care of the Earth.

→ **It seems that** people know they should take care of the Earth _____,
but they are not doing that.

2 People know they should not waste food.

→ _____,
but they are still doing it.

3 People know they should protect the environment.

→ _____,
but they are not doing that.

4 People know they should not pollute.

→ _____,
but they are still doing it.

B **Look at the example and write the sentences.**

1 | rivers and oceans / fill / with plastic waste |

→ Rivers and oceans **have been filled** with plastic waste. _____

2 | the fossil fuels / burn / to create energy |

→ _____

3 | almost half of the world's rainforests / destroy |

→ _____

4 | greenhouse gases / produce / by cows |

→ _____

26

C **Write the correct number in each blank. Then, write the sentences.**

1	These days, there are	_____	break down quickly
2	For instance, more and more people are using	_____	grow in some places
3	These items do not	_____	all kinds of environmental problems
4	Many fish and other marine life	_____	to grow crops as well
5	People put pesticides into the soil	_____	two major causes of pollution
6	Due to them, no plants can	_____	unsafe to drink, too
7	Pesticides are making the water supply	_____	plastic products these days
8	In conclusion, plastics and pesticides are	_____	are also dying because of this garbage

1 _____

2 _____

3 _____

4 _____

5 _____

6 _____

7 _____

8 _____

First Draft

Write the first draft by using the outline. Then, revise and edit your essay.

Title	
Introduction	
Body	
Conclusion	

Revising Checklist

1. Did you explain who is causing environmental problems in the introduction? ☐
2. Did you write two human activities that affect the environment? ☐
3. Did you use "It seems that ~" and "have/has been + p.p."? ☐

Editing Checklist   Capitalization ☐   Punctuation ☐   Grammar ☐   Spelling ☐

Final Draft

Write the final draft.

Title

Unit 8 Mobile Phones at Schools

A **Look at the example and write the sentences.**

1 (students / send text messages on their phones / play games on them)

→ Students **not only** send text messages on their phones **but also** play games on them.

2 (teens / get valuable work experience / learn how to deal with people)

→ _____

3 (class discussions / let students learn to speak better / make students more confident)

→ _____

4 (students / do not have to buy many clothes / do not worry about fashion)

→ _____

B **Look at the example and rewrite the sentences.**

1 They use their phones more. Their grades are worse.

→ **The more** they use their phones, **the worse** their grades are.

2 They talk in class more. Their speaking skills get better.

→ _____

3 They do more work. They get more work experience.

→ _____

4 They do more homework every day. They have more stress.

→ _____

C **Write the correct number in each blank. Then, write the sentences.**

1 But I do not agree that students should   _____ poorly in class

2 In fact, I believe that schools   _____ distracting me with their phones

3 So many students seem like they cannot   _____ they cause problems for others

4 When students use their mobile phones in class,   _____ should ban mobile phones

5 For example, I cannot focus   _____ use mobile phones at schools

6 I do not want students   _____ live without their phones

7 Schools need to ban   _____ on my lessons at times

8 They make students do   _____ mobile phones at once

1 _____

2 _____

3 _____

4 _____

5 _____

6 _____

7 _____

8 _____

First Draft

Write the first draft by using the outline. Then, revise and edit your essay.

Title	
Introduction	
Body	
Conclusion	

1. Did you explain whether you agree or disagree with a statement in the introduction? ☐
2. Did you write two reasons why you feel that way and their details? ☐
3. Did you use "not only A but also B" and "the + comparative, the + comparative?" ☐

Editing Checklist   Capitalization ☐   Punctuation ☐   Grammar ☐   Spelling ☐

Final Draft

Write the final draft.

Title _____

Memo

Memo